The Attitudes of Success

10 Powerful Habits of Successful, Confident Women

Sarah J. Collins

www.powerladieshub.com

Copyright © 2019 Sarah J. Collins.

All rights reserved. This book or any portion thereof may not be reproduced or used in any manner whatsoever without the express written permission of the publisher except for the use of brief quotations in a book review.

Printed by BrightSpark, Inc., in the United Kingdom.

www.powerladieshub.com

The Attitudes of Success

10 Powerful Habits of Successful, Confident Women

Contents

Introduction vii

Attitude 1: Command the Room 1

Attitude 2: Brand You 13

Attitude 3: Be Brave and Get Out of Your
   Comfort Zone 21

Attitude 4: Identify with a Successful Image 29

Attitude 5: Get Rid of Self-Doubt 36

Attitude 6: Build Influence 44

Attitude 7: Always Find New Opportunities
   to Learn 52

Attitude 8: Lead with Power 59

Attitude 9: Lose the Perfectionist Mentality 66

Attitude 10: Keep Going—Grit, Determination,
   and Perseverance 74

Final Note 82

Want more Success? 84

Introduction

> *"Your attitude, not your aptitude, will determine your altitude." – Zig Ziglar*

If you were asked to name some successful women, several names come to mind: Indra Nooyi, CEO of PepsiCo; Angela Merkel, Chancellor of Germany; Oprah Winfrey, TV presenter; Serena Williams, tennis champion; J. K. Rowling, author of the *Harry Potter* series. Each of these women has made it to the top of their field, yet, statistically, women in the workplace remain less likely than men to progress into the top jobs. In 2018, only twenty-four female CEOs were featured in the Fortune 500 list, and according to a 2017 Labor Force Survey carried out by the UK Office for National Statistics, women are more likely than men to work in low-paying sectors, a trend that extends across Europe. Why is this?

Well, as American author Zig Ziglar puts it, success is not down to aptitude alone, it's very much down to **attitude**.

Successful women have developed the right attitude to succeed, and powerful women have developed the right attitude to lead. In effect, women who reach the top of their game do so by developing an **attitude of success**. Attitude is everything, and *your* attitude determines *your* potential to succeed. The attitude you adopt influences not only your view of the world but also the way other people view you. Women often fall into a mental trap of believing that they are less successful than others simply because other women are better than themselves. In this book, you will learn that women who are successful are simply doing things *differently*. The unbelievable truth is that although these successful women do things differently, they share and adopt remarkably similar attitudes, and following their example will mean success for you, too.

Are you able to command a room and fill it with your presence? Do you constantly find yourself taking on too much and feeling unable to say no? Are your thoughts about yourself letting you down?

Women in leadership roles think positively, act positively, and make success a daily habit. You can, too. The contents of this book are designed to show you how by highlighting the **lessons we can learn from successful women.** These women all share successful habits but, like all habits, they can be learned and developed to help you build your own unstoppable attitude of success. The practical tips provided give you the kick start you need to begin the journey to achieving your true potential in the workplace. The powerful attitudes in this book are methods, techniques, and strategies that are practical, proven, and fast-acting. They are designed to give you the tools you need to change now, and you will find that each chapter focuses on specific actions you can take to bring you better, faster results, and make you a **power woman.**

When Marissa Mayer became CEO of Yahoo in 2012, she was the youngest woman ever to hold a leading role in a Fortune 500 company. Previously, she'd been the first female engineer employed at Google. In 1973, Hillary Clinton was one of only twenty-seven women to graduate from Yale Law School out of a class of 235. She then became the only woman on the team investigating President Nixon's impeachment. What attitude did Hillary have that made her different? Why did she achieve success when there were other women just like her, or others even more knowledgeable than her, who didn't? Each chapter contains examples of the methods employed by successful women, providing you with the inspiration and encouragement you need to achieve your own success. You don't need to read the attitudes in order; start with the one you think you need the most. You'll find lots of actionable tips and tricks in each chapter's 'Try This' section, and every tip is designed to fit into your life daily life. The more you do, the better you'll get.

Women today are beginning to break through "glass ceilings", but many of those in leadership roles believe that a fear of success is yet another invisible barrier holding women back. The problem with this fear is that it limits or prevents action, but time and again, studies have found that action and perseverance are the most essential elements of achieving success. It takes focused action to succeed in any field, and intelligence, education and skills will always take a backseat to persistence.

As a thank you for buying this book, you will receive a bonus guide with detailed steps showing you the secrets of the most productive women. These are actionable steps that you can use immediately to help you get more out of everything you do. Simply use the link provided at the end of the first chapter to download the guide. Throughout this book, you will also find links to websites and videos that will help you to visualize and stay focused on the attitude you need to develop.

We each have the potential to succeed in whatever we put our minds to if we learn how to develop and adopt the habits and attitudes of successful women—simple habits that will have an instant impact on the way you think and act and the way you are perceived by others. Remember, the key to success is action. Are you ready to put these attitudes to work? The sooner you learn and apply them, the sooner you will move in the direction of becoming a power woman. Let the stories in this book inspire you and, most importantly, let the strategies and tips you learn transform you into a successful woman.

Success is an attitude. Are you ready to elevate yours?

ATTITUDE 1:

Command the Room

> *"A strong, confident person can rule the room with knowledge, personal style, attitude, and great posture."* — Cindy Ann Peterson

Cindy Ann Peterson is an independent fashion, design, and image consultant who has worked with many high-profile clients, helping them to command the room wherever they go. She knows that *what* you say is often overshadowed by *how* you say it, and that both your body language and the way you carry yourself speak volumes about your confidence and the way you feel about yourself.

Body Language

It's often said that communication is 55 percent body language, 38 percent tone of voice, and only 7 percent spoken word, but these figures come from research carried out by Albert Mehrabian in the early 1970s that was never intended to be used as a hard-and-fast rule in every situation. Today, however, experts generally agree that approximately 60 percent of daily communication is verbal and the remaining 40 percent is nonverbal, including body language and tone of voice. Allan and Barbara Pease, the authors of *The Definitive Book of Body Language*, believe that, in a business environment, 60–80 percent of the impact made in a meeting or around a negotiating table comes down to body language. We use words to say what we want others to hear, but it's the tone of voice and body language we use as we speak that helps to convey deeper meaning and intent. The authors also believe that women are better than men at reading body language, and research carried out by psychologists at Harvard University has demonstrated that "women's intuition" is an innate skill, making women more perceptive of nonverbal cues.

The American actress Mae West once said, "I speak two languages: body and English." In the 1930s, her fame as an actress, comedian, singer, screenwriter, and playwright was growing, and she certainly knew how to command a room. Her posture, attitude, and tone of voice all helped to convey her Hollywood star status, but commanding a room is not about making a big noise—it's about learning how to use verbal *and* nonverbal communication to project a professional image and convey status in any environment, including the workplace.

Confident women command a room by ...

Making eye contact with and acknowledging other people in the room. To command a room, others in the room need to know you're there. If you enter quietly without saying a word, your presence in the room may go completely unnoticed. It's not about being loud and drawing attention to yourself in a potentially negative way; simply acknowledge others with a smile, a nod of your head, or a wave of your hand when appropriate. When you acknowledge others, they in turn acknowledge you, but you also make them feel important, which helps to foster mutual respect.

Positioning themselves to be seen and to see others. Where you sit in a room is important. If you position yourself in a quiet corner or on the sidelines, you instantly present yourself as being less important than others in the room. To command the room, you need to sit where you can be seen by others *and* where you can engage with others. You're not there to make up the numbers; you're there to take part in the proceedings, so choose a central position. Facebook COO Sheryl Sandberg puts it this way: "Don't expect that you'll get to the corner office by sitting on the sidelines. Women need to sit at the table."

Using their posture, attitude, and tone of voice to make their presence known. Again, it's not about making a big noise, it's about making a positive impact. Confident women sit or stand with a confident posture, occupying their space in the room and using open body language to invite others to engage with them rather than closing themselves off with a guarded posture such as folded arms. They actively contribute to discussions and conversations without asking for permission to interject, especially when they have expert knowledge on a topic, and they never apologize for having something to say.

Social psychologist Amy Cuddy believes that open, expansive postures such as standing with your hands on your hips (think Wonder Woman) or sitting with your arms up and hands laced behind your head create the impression of being bigger, thereby creating a bigger presence in a room. The key finding in her research into body language and power is that adopting expansive postures makes us *feel* more powerful, more confident, and more assertive, and we are therefore perceived as being more powerful by others. This feeling of power also makes us speak more slowly. We're in control of what we say and how we say it, so we effectively expand the speaking space we have, which helps us to share ideas more openly. She says, "When we feel powerful, we expand. When we feel powerless, we shrink."

Listening to others.

Being able to listen is an important communication skill, and giving others your undivided attention when they speak is the only way to encourage them to extend the same courtesy to you. If you show an interest in others, they will show an interest in you, but learning how to command a room comes down to knowing when to speak and when to listen—letting your body language do the talking for you.

Commanding with charisma.

Mae West had charismatic charm, as did Marilyn Monroe and Princess Diana. They all shared an ability to express themselves through body language and to command attention without saying a word, but charismatic people don't hog the limelight, they are skilled at letting other people know they matter.

If you want to command a room, what you say is important. No one is going to listen if you have nothing relevant or of interest to say, but getting your message across requires a confident delivery. Remember, "A strong, confident person can rule the room with knowledge, personal style, attitude, and great posture." Nonverbal communication is equally important.

Try This

Begin by making a study of your own body language. The way you feel comes across in your body language. Most of your gestures and movements will be subconscious, so become more aware of the body language you use. You already know how you feel, so begin to make connections between your commonly used body language and your emotions. For example, pay attention to what you do with your hands when you're in a meeting, and note whether you cross your legs or fold your arms.

Next, study inspirational role models. Take a look at the people you admire. What messages do they communicate through their body language? Watch them in action. Observe their posture, their facial expressions, and their hand gestures—everything that helps them to come across as the person you admire.

Then, make notes and compare. What do women who command a room do differently to you? Knowledge is power. Use what you learn to begin developing your own effective body language through mirroring their example, taking care not to get too caught up in observing others as it's important to create your own style.

And finally, to build your confidence as you learn to use more open, expansive body language, try **power posing.** Amy Cuddy believes that adopting a powerful pose such as standing tall with feet apart and hands on hips for two minutes can give your confidence a powerful boost. She recommends standing in this expansive posture for two minutes prior to taking part in any event that requires you to feel and be seen as confident, powerful, and assertive.

Use the **steepling** gesture. In his studies of body movements, the anthropologist Ray Birdwhistell found that powerful politicians, lawyers, and executives gave instructions while using this power position. You can achieve this position by separating your palms slightly with fingertips lightly touching each other to making a little rooftop, like the steeple on a building. This is how this hand position looks like.

What You Say: What Leadership and Confidence Sounds Like

- **Don't pose your statements as questions!** Minimize your "upspeak." Women's voices sometimes rise at the end of a sentence as if they're asking a question. Posing statements as questions makes you appear less confident, and opens the door for people to dismiss your ideas. Every time you find yourself presenting your ideas as questions, stop and change them into statements.

Instead of saying, "Do you think we should … ?," start saying, "I recommend we …" Leveling your voice through practice can therefore help you become more authoritative.

- **Stop using filler words.** Words like "um," "ah," and "you know"—these are all words that are known as hesitation or filler words. We use them for a number of reasons: to fill a silence or out of habit. The problem with them is that they make you sound less confident and in control. Awareness is the key to avoiding these words. Begin recording yourself when you're talking to family or friends so that you can hear what you sound like in everyday conversations. This is the best way to become aware of filler words you use. When you hear yourself say one, backtrack and replace it with the word you actually mean to say, or repeat the last couple of words without the filler word. The more you do this, the quicker you'll train your mind away from them.

- **Quit saying "sorry" so much.** Constantly apologizing can give the appearance of incompetence. To stop this pattern, count the number of times you apologize when you do not need to. Start to identify triggers that worsen the behavior, such as certain people, contexts, moods, or times of the day. Pay attention to whether your tendency to over apologize comes out with some coworkers more than others. Start replacing needless apologies with accurate statements to communicate your point.

- **Own your accomplishments.** Do not downplay them. Do not respond to a compliment by saying, "It was only … ," or "Oh, thanks, but I just helped out a little bit—it was no big deal." Practice saying, "Thank you, I'm really happy with how it turned out." Keep practicing how you will respond to compliments and congratulations, and it will soon roll off your tongue.

- **Don't talk too quickly.** People interpret fast-talking as a sign of both nervousness and a lack of self-confidence. Talking too quickly can give off the impression that you don't think people want to listen to you, or that what you have to say is not important

FREE E-BOOK!

Here is the link to the free e-book on the guide to most productive women as promised.

http://www.powerladieshub.com/free-bonus/

Also visit our website www.powerladieshub.com for more excellent resources.

ATTITUDE 2:

Brand You

"Do not desire to fit in. Desire to lead."
—Mary Kay Ash

In 1999, Mary Kay Ash was awarded the title of Most Outstanding Woman in Business in the 20th Century by Lifetime Television. Today, she's considered America's greatest woman entrepreneur, but it all began back in 1963 when Mary Kay realized that she no longer desired to fit in; she dared to lead.

Mary Kay Cosmetics, Inc., was founded with an investment of $5,000 and a salesforce of only nine women. According to the latest figures, the company now has an estimated value of approximately

$2.6 billion, and the number of independent beauty consultants selling Mary Kay products has grown to over 3.5 million operating in 35 global markets. Mary Kay Ash founded her company on a desire to lead and to forge a path for women to succeed in what she viewed to be a male-dominated business world.

Desire to Lead

Mary Kay the brand became a reflection of Mary Kay the person. Your personal brand image must reflect *your* core values and beliefs, but all power women began building their brand on shared principles, and you can adopt and apply the same strategies to developing your own brand:

Take credit for *your* achievements. Unless you're prepared to showcase your skills and abilities in the workplace, your achievements may go completely unnoticed, or credit for them may be claimed by someone else. Get comfortable with taking full credit for *your* achievements and speak up when your efforts are being overlooked.

Don't be too modest. No one makes it to the top of their game on their own, and arrogance is not an attractive character trait, but it is possible to be too modest. If you're unwilling to take credit where it's due, you risk being seen by others as a follower rather than a leader. Actively seek opportunities to showcase your skills and speak up about your successes; otherwise, you may find yourself overlooked. If you don't believe in your abilities, who will?

Don't give away your ideas. Believe in your ideas in the same way you believe in yourself. Mary Kay put her name on her idea and turned it into a business that reflected her core values and beliefs. Her idea paved the way for millions of other women to succeed, but she didn't give it away.

Brand You

A brand is simply a recognizable name, design, or symbol that makes the thing it represents stand out from other things. It might be a product or a company, but either way, people buy into the brand because it represents what that product or company stands for—their brand is their reputation. When building a personal brand, you're building your own recognizable image that will make you stand out from the crowd and represents the value you offer in your field.

If you're an entrepreneur building a business, your target audience needs to know what your business is and what it can offer them. They also need to know what makes your offering different to your competition's offerings—what makes you a better choice for them? If you're looking for promotion in your current workplace or planning to move into a new career, the departments responsible for hiring new talent need to know who you are, what you can offer them, and what makes you the best choice for them. This is where a strong personal brand can help you to stand out as the person they need.

Strong Personal Brands

Power women have strong personal brands. No matter what their field, they all promote what they represent and what they do best through their brand,

and they make those brands strong by being these three things:

1. **Authentic**

   Angela Merkel is a perfect example of woman who has cultivated a strong, authentic personal brand. She is currently at the top of *Forbes*'s World's 100 Most Powerful Women list, but her personal brand is just as powerful as her political status. Her hardworking, practical, unglamorous image made her unpopular with some people early in her career, but instead of changing her image to suit her critics, she used it to promote her pragmatic, down-to-earth approach to leadership. Successful business brands are built on consistency, and it takes a consistent, authentic personal brand to build the same success.

2. **Different**

   Successful women do things differently. Facebook COO Sheryl Sandberg offers a great example of taking something that already exists and making it your own by approaching it differently. With her call to *lean in,* she promoted women's leadership in her own unique way. She advised women to bring their whole selves to work, not just their public or professional persona, meaning they should drop the commonly held opinion that to get ahead in the workplace they would need to adopt a stereotypically "male" approach—being aggressive and never showing vulnerability. By boldly pointing out that women often hold themselves back in the workplace by not believing in themselves and their abilities as women *and* leaders, she did something that no other high-profile woman in business had done before her. Her personal brand has inspired many more women to follow her lead.

3. Visible

No matter how good your offering or how different your approach, no one is going to know about it unless you make yourself visible. A strong business brand is a recognized brand, and a strong personal brand makes you stand out. During her years at Google, Marissa Mayer became the public face of the company. She rose through the ranks, creating a strong personal brand as an "articulate geek," giving her a unique edge.

Try This

In the business world, companies need a strong brand to stand out from the crowd. The same principles can be applied to creating your own personal brand. Brand You is who you are, what you have to offer, and what you stand for.

Begin by understanding who you are to understand your value. Sit down and write out a list of everything you're good at. What skills do you have? What tasks do you excel at? What unique experiences have helped shape your skills and expertise? What makes you different? You need to know what you have to offer to know what needs you can address and where you can offer the most value.

Next, know what you stand for. Put your core values into words. What drives your career ambitions? What matters most in business and in the workplace? What personal attributes do you value most? It's important that the person you believe yourself to be matches the person others believe you to be. Sticking to your values in your words and your actions makes you an authentic "brand" that can be trusted.

Then, be the best. When you know who you are, what you offer, and what you stand for, be the best in every aspect. Never stop striving to be a better you, both personally and professionally. Knowledge is power, so build your brand by building your knowledge and your self-confidence. Desire to lead, *be* the leader you want to be. Be bold, be different, and be visible by doing what you do better than anyone else. As Anita Roddick, founder of the Body Shop once said, "If you do things well, do them better."

ATTITUDE 3:

Be Brave and Get Out of Your Comfort Zone

"Do one thing every day that scares you."
—*Eleanor Roosevelt*

Eleanor Roosevelt was considered outspoken in her years as First Lady of the United States, but she redefined the role, paving the way for those who followed her to have an independent voice in the White House. By pushing boundaries and stepping out beyond her predefined role, she became a globally admired and powerful woman. Her forthright attitude was perhaps best summed up when she said, "A woman is like a tea bag—you can't tell how strong she is until you put her in hot water."

Being Nice

The world has changed in many ways since Eleanor Roosevelt's day, but for many women in the workplace today, the one thing that scares them every day is saying "no." This fear can stem from a variety of sources, including the desire to keep your options open by being involved, hoping to be considered a team player by your colleagues, or wanting to please a boss, but often it's simply because saying no makes you feel uncomfortable.

However, saying yes to every request in the workplace can quickly backfire. Many women find themselves conditioned to say yes because it's the "nice" thing to do, but taking on too many projects will eventually have a negative effect on your productivity and the quality of your work. You may be considered nice, but if you're missing deadlines, you may also be considered unreliable. This subconscious conditioning is something Facebook Chief Operating

Officer Sheryl Sandberg believes is holding women back, and she speaks from personal experience in the workplace.

Lean In

In 2008, Sheryl Sandberg stepped into the new role of COO at Facebook after several years as Vice President of Global Online Sales and Operations at Google. She had already earned a place on *Forbes*'s World's 100 Most Powerful Women list, yet in her first performance review with Facebook CEO Mark Zuckerberg, he commented that her desire to be nice and to be liked by everyone was holding her back, saying, "Pleasing everyone won't change anything." This echoes Mary Kay Ash's belief that women should not desire to fit in but rather to lead, and in 2013, Sandberg published *Lean In: Women, Work, and the Will to Lead.* One of the controversial points raised by Sandberg in her book is that women's fear of success stems from a fear of not being liked. Observing that men who achieve success are liked and admired whereas successful women are less well liked, she remarks, "Everyone needs to get more comfortable with female leaders, including female leaders themselves."

Step Out

Getting comfortable with being a leader means getting comfortable with stepping out of your comfort zone. Learning how to say no and move on without guilt is the first step towards getting comfortable with being uncomfortable.

Be clear on what matters most. Before saying yes to a request, consider whether the project you're being asked to take on matters to *you*. There are only so many hours in a day, so your time and energy must be focused on projects that are important to you and your career. Saying no is a balancing act. Weigh up the amount of work involved, the time required, and the deadline you're being asked to commit to, and only say yes if your efforts would lead to personal satisfaction and professional reward.

Be prepared to say no. Suzi Welch is a business journalist and management author who has helped many women to avoid the trap of saying yes when they know they should say no. She recommends having a list of responses ready so that you're prepared to say no without feeling uncomfortable.

For example, "Thanks for thinking of me, but I'm overscheduled to a fault right now," is a good response when the request isn't one that weighs up in terms of personal satisfaction or professional reward. Or, "Thanks for thinking of me, but I can assure you there is someone far more appropriate than me for that job," can be useful if you know the request is not a good fit for your skill set and therefore wouldn't provide an opportunity to showcase your abilities.

Be honest. Honesty is always the best policy and authenticity is always the way to earn respect. In some work environments, the fear of repercussions can lead to fabricating excuses to justify the need to say no; however, lies will inevitably catch up with you. Being caught out will lead to others seeing you as untrustworthy and unreliable, so a simple, candid explanation is always best. For example, Suzi suggests, "No, I'm afraid I have a family obligation that I just can't get out of."

Adjust Your Mind-set

Psychologist Carol Dweck is the author of *Mindset: The New Psychology of Success*, and after decades of research, she believes that adopting a growth mind-set holds the key to achieving success in all areas of life. In a growth mind-set, you believe that change is always possible and that you have unlimited potential to achieve more. In comparison, a fixed mind-set keeps you stuck where you are, held back by the belief that your situation can't be changed.

In both her personal and business life, Sheryl Sandberg has struggled with self-doubt on many occasions. She knows that fear can keep you trapped in your comfort zone and prevent you from realizing your true potential, but she has learned to silence the voices of doubt in her mind by asking herself, "What would I do if I weren't afraid?" In doing so, she has learned to adopt a growth mind-set. Power women push themselves to achieve more by consistently stepping out of their comfort zones. They *all* have a growth mind-set, so the key to achieving your own success lies in learning to do the same.

Try This

Be brave and step out of your comfort zone by learning how to adopt a growth mind-set.

Learn to hear your fixed mind-set "voice." In a fixed mind-set, your inner voice of self-doubt may be saying, "You're not good enough to do this," or "Don't even try it, you'll only mess up."

Recognize that you have a choice. The way you interpret a challenging situation is entirely *your* choice. Recognize that the negative voice in your head doesn't have all the answers and you don't need to listen to it.

Talk back with a growth mind-set voice. Your fixed mind-set voice may be asking, "What if you fail?," but you can reply with a growth mind-set voice and say, "What if I succeed?" Tell yourself that most successful people experienced failures along the way, and choose to focus on the potential for success.

Take the growth mind-set action. The process of learning to override the fixed mind-set voice and drown it out with a growth mind-set voice will take time, but the choice of how to deal with challenges and setbacks is ultimately yours to make. Take control.

ATTITUDE 4:

Identify with a Successful Image

> *"People seldom improve when they have no other model but themselves to copy."*
> *—Oliver Goldsmith*

When successful women are asked if they have a role model or image they identify with, the answer is always "yes." In recent interviews, Oprah Winfrey named Maya Angelou as a role model, Oscar nominee Jessica Chastain named fellow actress Isabelle Huppert, and Michelle Obama named Eleanor Roosevelt. But when they were asked to give reasons for their choices, it became clear that even though these role models have found success in their chosen careers, that's not what makes them ideal role models—it's their attitude.

Do We Need Role Models?

A good role model is someone you can look up to, someone with values you admire, someone whose thoughts and actions you want to emulate—someone you think of when facing a challenging situation, asking yourself, "What would they do?" We *do* need role models, but the aim must always be to find a role model who inspires us to become better versions of ourselves—the best we can possibly be.

A positive role model can act as a guide, helping you to understand the actions you can take to become the person you want to be, and the attitude you need to adopt to achieve your goals. This means that the ideal role model for you is someone who possesses the character traits you will need to get you from where you are now to where you want to be.

Becoming Your Best Self

People seldom improve when they have no other model but themselves to copy. The role models chosen by the successful women listed above all have character traits and attitudes they admire and aspire to emulate—not so that they can become carbon copies of those individuals, but rather better versions of themselves.

Those traits include:

- Optimism
- Confidence
- Passion
- Humility
- Integrity
- Tenacity
- Respect

Oprah Winfrey admired Maya Angelou's positive outlook on life and lifelong zeal for learning. Jessica

Chastain admired Isabelle Huppert's willingness to step out of her comfort zone and try new things. Michelle Obama admired Eleanor Roosevelt's forthright attitude and determination to push boundaries by speaking up for those struggling to make their voices heard. Becoming your best self is all about identifying the characteristics and attitudes you will need to achieve your goals, and then learning through the example of others who possess those attributes.

The Ripple of Influence

Identifying with a role model is not about trying to achieve their success; it's about getting into their mind and discovering the everyday thought processes, actions, and habits that have allowed them to succeed, and developing the same attitudes to pursue your own success.

Dame Kelly Holmes is a role model for many aspiring athletes. They might follow her training program, her diet plan, and wear her chosen brand of sports clothing, but unless they understand the thoughts and beliefs that drive her actions and the strengths in her character that allow her to overcome setbacks and injury, their dream of matching her Olympic success is unlikely to become their reality. Dame Kelly is an inspirational role model, but it takes an understanding of her mental strengths as well as her physical strengths to understand what is required to achieve Olympic gold.

Role models inspire the success of others, but those role models also have role models, and those they inspire may go on to become role models themselves. In the same way that a pebble dropped into a pond creates ripples that reach ever outwards, the ripple of influence can spread far and wide through an inspirational role model. It's not about being famous; it's all about demonstrating the character strengths that others aspire to call their own. Parents and relatives can be positive role models for children. Teachers and coaches can be positive role models for students, and friends and work colleagues can be role models for one another on many levels.

Try This

Here are five things you can do today to identify with a successful image:

1. **Ask yourself: What do you value most?** Take time to consider the core values that guide your decisions in life and make you the person you are or want to be. Write them down.

2. **Next, ask yourself:** To live by these values and be the person you want to be every hour of every day, what character traits and attributes do you need to have? Write them down.

3. **Look at your lists and identify people you know who already demonstrate those values and possess those traits.** These may be people you know personally or people you admire from afar. It may not be possible to identify one person who offers the whole package, so create a list of people and note the attributes they have that make them a good role model for you.

4. **Make a study of these individuals.** Look beyond their success and accomplishments to learn as much as possible about their daily lives and routines. Observe them, read about them, listen to them talk. What beliefs, thoughts, and emotions drive their actions? What events have helped shape them into the people they are today? What motivates them on a day-to-day basis? How do they deal with setbacks? Who are their role models? How do they interact with other people in daily life?

5. **Find ways to connect.** Spending time with positive people is both inspirational and motivational. Find ways to spend time with and be around the positive role models you know or look for ways to connect through social media. The more you know about the people you admire, the more you learn about what makes them tick. Use what you learn to become a better you and to achieve your own success.

ATTITUDE 5:

Get Rid of Self-Doubt

"When you doubt your power, you give power to your doubt."—Honoré de Balzac

---

It's natural to experience self-doubt from time to time, but according to executive coach Janet Ioli, women are particularly prone to doubting themselves and their abilities at every stage in their careers—even when they make it all the way to the top. Many high achievers with solid track records of success continue to struggle with self-doubt. It can manifest as feelings of being unqualified for one's job or undeserving of praise or accolades, or as a fear of being "found out" as a fraud, and it's known as impostor syndrome.

Exercise Your Confidence Muscles

Poet and author Maya Angelou often spoke of feelings of inadequacy and of being "found out," actress Emma Watson has spoken in interviews about her experiences with crippling self-doubt and insecurity, and Facebook COO Sheryl Sandberg has spoken openly many times about her struggles with lacking self-confidence. "Confidence and leadership are muscles," she said. "You learn to use them or not to." What she means by this is that every time you do something that makes you uncomfortable, such as speaking up in a meeting or taking your place at the conference table rather than sitting on the sidelines, you exercise your confidence muscles and they will get stronger as a result. If you don't use them, just like the muscles in your body, they become weaker.

Alison Wagonfeld is Vice President of Marketing for Google Cloud. In her career, she's had to exercise her confidence muscles to help her deal with self-doubt in meetings. "In group discussions, like board meetings and investment team meetings, I try to speak up in the first 15 minutes," she says. "If I get involved in the conversation early, I feel more confident contributing throughout." She has also learned to be mindful of the language she uses, both spoken and written. "I'm sorry" is now a phrase she tries to avoid. She believes that apologizing puts her in a less confident state of mind, whether it's apologizing for speaking up at a meeting or beginning an email with an apology for not responding sooner.

Former vice president of Adobe Systems Karen Catlin turns to her V gmyth-busting posse" when she finds herself in the grips of imposter syndrome: "These are the people I can be vulnerable with, those I confide in when I'm lacking confidence." Her myth-busting posse helps her to fend off insecurities by reminding her of her accomplishments and the reasons why her success is deserved.

Forgive Mistakes

Self-doubt leads many women to judge themselves harshly and set impossible, unrealistic expectations for themselves to achieve perfection in everything they do. Mistakes made are therefore considered to be confirmation of their inadequacy, creating an ongoing cycle of doubt and self-criticism.

Jessica Lawrence Quinn is the founder of NY Tech Meetup. She believes that the best way to deal with mistakes is to remember that *everyone* messes up at some point, and that the mistakes you make don't define who you are. Mistakes are only failures if you fail to learn from them and take the positives forward with you as you move on. "Part of performing at your peak," she says, "is forgiving yourself when you're not—and moving on." This means adopting a growth mind-set and accepting that a less-than-perfect performance today does not mean that you can't learn, adapt, improve, and do better tomorrow:

- An unproductive day at your desk doesn't mean that you're a lazy, unproductive person; you can do more tomorrow.

- A talk that doesn't go as planned or achieve the desired outcome doesn't mean that you're a poor speaker; you can learn and improve.

- One failure at closing a sale doesn't make you a failure as a salesperson.

Self-doubt and fear of failure go hand in hand. When you doubt your abilities, you fear stepping out of your comfort zone, so any failure experienced when you do step out will often spiral quickly into thoughts of giving up. This was something Dona Sarkar, now a lead software engineer at Microsoft, experienced in her first year at the University of Michigan. She had less coding experience than others in the computer science program, but she was reluctant to ask questions out of a fear of exposing her limited knowledge: "I was so afraid to go up and ask questions because one of the guys had made a comment about girls being airheads." Trying to muddle through on her own resulted in her failing the class, and Sarkar gave serious consideration to dropping out of the program completely. She talked herself out of it, however, and repeated the class, this time passing. "I told myself, this is my dream and I'm not going to let one failure hold me back. … I cried a bunch, said I'd never do it again, then I got back on two days later and did fine."

> *"Try something. Fail. And do it again."*
> —Dona Sarkar

Celebrate Every Win

When thoughts of doubt are at the forefront of your mind, it's all too easy to focus only on failure and the things that don't quite go to plan. In those moments, believing that things always go wrong for you or that you're not deserving of success gives power to your doubt.

Celebrating every win is a powerful way of breaking the negative cycle of self-doubt and building an attitude of success. Every success, no matter how small, should be celebrated in some way so that a bank of positive experiences and accomplishments can be drawn on to help combat negativity and self-doubt when it threatens to stop you in your tracks. Psychologist Adam Grant encouraged Sheryl Sandberg to use this approach when her confidence hit rock bottom after the sudden death of her husband. He suggested that she should get into the habit of writing down three positive things about her day before going to bed each night. These positives should be small achievements or things that she had done well that day. "Some days, I had such a hard time thinking of anything I did well that I'd end up listing 'Made a cup of tea,'" Sandberg says. "But over time, focusing on things I'd done well helped me rebuild my confidence. Even if it was small, I could record something positive each day."

Try This

To help deal with feelings of self-doubt, take the advice of experts and learn from the hands-on experiences of women who have found ways to take the power away from their doubt.

Accentuate the positives: On an index card, write down the talents, strengths, and attributes you possess that have helped you to succeed. Keep the card with you and look at it whenever self-doubt creeps into your mind or whenever failure leaves you feeling like giving up.

Grow your own myth-busting posse: Follow Karen Catlin's advice and identify your own "myth-busting posse." These might be friends or relatives who know you well, or work colleagues who know your strengths, talents, and abilities. Whenever you're having a confidence crisis, let their encouragement help silence the negative voices of doubt in your mind.

Start journaling: Expand on Sheryl Sandberg's habit of writing down three positive things at the end of each day by starting a journal. Scientific research has shown that developing a habit of journaling positive experiences helps to boost the release of feel-good endorphins because the writing process allows the events to be relived through memory. The self-esteem boost this creates can then be recalled whenever doubt creeps to the forefront of your mind.

ATTITUDE 6:

Build Influence

> *"The key to successful leadership today is influence, not authority."* —Ken Blanchard

To succeed in any field, you need influence. When you have influence, your point of view is listened to and your ideas are considered worthy of attention. However, according to Kathryn Heath, coauthor of *The Influence Effect*, women in the workplace find it harder than men to build influence. "Studies show that imitating male characteristics doesn't translate to professional advancement for women," she says. "We women do not like unbridled competition, backroom deals, or trading favors. We favor collaboration, inclusion, and win–win outcomes. The distinctive missing link is influence."

Begin Building

Krystal Covington is a marketing consultant with a special interest in workplace influence. Her research has uncovered three key areas around which influence can be built.

Presence. We've all heard the expressions "dress to impress" and "look the part," and in terms of building influence, the way you present yourself matters. However, creating a powerful presence goes beyond clothing to include body language and the way you interact with others. "Our presence is both the way we walk into a room and the clothes we wear on our bodies," Krystal says. "It's the first thing people judge when they see us and dictates a huge part of the impressions we make."

Reputation. To build a good reputation, you need to be credible. Gaining qualifications in your field is one way to boost credibility, but demonstrating relevant experience and ability is just as important. In Attitude 2, you learned the value of creating your own personal brand to stand out from the crowd, but your brand image can also help to grow your reputation, promoting who you are and what you stand for.

Visibility. In the same way that being visible is an essential element of building a personal brand, you need to get your ideas out there to be considered worthy of attention. The more visible and consistent you are in the way you present yourself and your ideas, the more trusted and influential you become.

The Power of Networking

It stands to reason that knowing a lot of people gives you greater power to influence simply because you have more people to share information with. Research in the field of power and influence has shown that networking *can* build influence, but doing so is dependent on building relationships with people within the network. Influencing someone you know will always be easier than influencing a stranger, and it's for this reason that social networks such as Facebook have been found less effective than face-to-face meetings in terms of building trust. Your power to influence depends on the strength of your network relationships, and the strength of those relationships will depend largely on the amount of time you've devoted to developing the three key areas of presence, reputation, and visibility.

An excellent example of the power of networking can be found in Christine Lagarde. She was the first woman to hold the position of finance minister in France and she is the first to become managing director of the International Monetary Fund. Her experience gave her the credentials she needed to be considered for the role, but highly successful women proactively promote themselves through carefully planned marketing and networking campaigns; they leave nothing to chance. Christine used the power of networking across the globe to ensure she would have the support she needed to secure the position she wanted.

The greater your presence, reputation, and visibility, the greater your potential to influence others. People need to know who you are and what skills or expertise you have before they can judge your value as a network partner. There's also a great deal of truth in the saying, "It's not what you know, it's who you know," because the more powerful, influential people in your network and the more frequently you connect with them, the more opportunities you gain to build your reputation and influence through those connections.

Building Relationships to Build Influence

The connections you make can also help you to identify potential mentors. The right mentor for you will have the right mix of skills and experience to help you achieve your goals, but essential qualities include empathy, honesty, and superior communication skills. These qualities can only be identified through building personal relationships.

"If I hadn't had mentors, I wouldn't be here today. I'm a product of great mentoring, great coaching. …

Coaches or mentors are very important." — Indra Nooyi, CEO, PepsiCo

Developing your communication skills enhances your ability to build meaningful relationships. The better your connection with people on a personal level, the greater your power to influence.

Celeste Headlee is a radio broadcaster who believes everyone can benefit from taking the time to hone their interpersonal conversational skills. In her popular TED Talk, she offers the following pointers.

Don't multitask. Give the person you're talking to your full attention.

Listen. Listening is a skill, and it is just as important as talking in terms of communication skills.

Go with the flow. Allow a conversation to take its course; it's not a script.

Use open-ended questions. Show genuine interest in others and they'll show interest in you.

It's okay to say you don't know. Don't pretend to be an expert when you're not; authenticity is key to building trust.

With well-honed communication skills, you have the capacity to make others feel important. Everyone likes to feel valued and accepted, and your influence goes a long way when others feel important in your presence.

Try This

Build connections. Building influence begins with building connections. Dorie Clark, author of *Entrepreneurial You*, says, "At a fundamental level, one of the reasons that people do things for you—support your idea, or approve your budget—is because they like you." Building connections is all about building rapport with your colleagues and the people you interact with regularly.

Develop expertise. Build your knowledge, immerse yourself in the latest research, attend conferences, and build your reputation as an expert in your field. Become the go-to person on that topic in your network.

Stay visible. Keep networking and growing your connections. The more you put yourself out there, the more opportunity you have to build influence.

ATTITUDE 7:

Always Find New Opportunities to Learn

"Leadership and learning are indispensable to each other."—John F. Kennedy

It's often said that knowledge is power, but it's also said that you can't know what you don't know. From these two sayings, the need for ongoing learning becomes clear. In terms of developing your personal and professional knowledge, however, it's important to set some parameters to provide focus in your learning. To get started, consider your answers to the following questions:

- What are you interested in? Interest provides motivation.

- Where do you want your new knowledge to take you?

- What will you need to learn to bridge the gap between where you are now and where you want to be?

Finding new opportunities to learn becomes much easier once you've established what you want to gain from furthering your skills and knowledge.

Benefits of Learning

Successful women adopt a learning mind-set, meaning they are always open to and actively looking for new opportunities to learn. They view intelligence, whether academic or skills-based, as endless, and they know that there is always something new to learn—no one knows everything. If nothing else, ongoing learning is essential to keeping up with the latest advances in technology in today's fast-paced world. Studies have shown, however, that learning brings with it the added benefits of boosting confidence and building resilience. The experience of challenging oneself to learn something new creates confidence, and ongoing learning develops greater resilience not only through completing the task but also through solving problems along the way.

Learning Opportunities

As adults, learning is all too often considered too time-consuming or no longer relevant to the real world. This is because learning is associated with schools and classrooms, but learning can take many other forms.

Reading. Knowledge is power. The more you know about the field you work in or aspire to work in, the greater your potential to become a leading expert in your field. At any level in the workplace, reading industry-related books, magazines, or websites keeps you on the cutting edge, increasing your networking value and building your reputation.

Listening. The more time you spend listening to people who have greater knowledge or experience than you, the greater your opportunity to learn from them.

Knowing what you don't know. It's only by accepting that you don't know everything that you can remain open to learning new things. Having the confidence to admit to gaps in your knowledge or understanding allows you to look for appropriate resources or experts to help you learn.

Acting. Reading and listening aren't enough. Success in any field depends on being able to put what you've learned into practice.

Teaching. Passing on your knowledge is a proven way of reinforcing your own learning.

Seeking a mentor. When you learn through a mentor, you learn through the experience of someone else. There have been many high-profile mentor–mentee relationships, but mentors can be found in all areas of life, not just in your chosen field.

Learning through Experience

During her years as CEO at Yahoo!, Marissa Mayer continued to develop her leadership skills not only through building relationships with mentors, but also through keeping lines of communication open across every department and at every level in the company. She wanted to learn from the ideas and experiences of employees and then share those ideas in the boardroom. While her leadership style and overall performance at Yahoo! has been the subject of much debate, her openness to learning from every source is an essential attitude in terms of growing as a leader. "One of the best pieces of advice I've ever gotten is there are always a lot of good choices, and then there's the one you pick, commit to, and make great," she says.

Not every decision you make is guaranteed to be a great one, but there are always lessons to be learned from every outcome. Life is learning, and learning through experience is proof positive that you're trying new things and growing as a person.

Try This

To help you identify the best areas of focus for your ongoing learning, experts suggest creating a personal SWOT analysis. On a sheet of paper, draw lines to create four columns—Strengths, Weaknesses, Opportunities, and Threats.

Strengths: In this column, list your skills, qualifications, talents, experience, personal qualities, and anything else you consider to be a strength.

Weaknesses: In this column, list any areas you believe need to be addressed or improved to help you move forward in your career.

Opportunities: In this column, list potential sources of new learning that could help you to build your strengths, including formal training, informal networking, possible mentors, knowledge sharing, independent study, and so on.

Threats: In this column, list any factors or potential barriers in your environment that could get in the way of progress, limit your learning, or hold you back in any way.

Armed with this analysis, you now have the information you need to help you find new opportunities to learn and to make the most of the opportunities that are all around you every day. Knowledge is power, and power women are lifelong learners.

ATTITUDE 8:

Lead with Power

"The most effective way to do it, is to do it."
—Amelia Earhart

An effective leader leads through the ability to influence others, and power adds to influence. The overall success of a leader ultimately depends on their ability to get things done, but it's their leadership style and the power base they operate from that determines how well liked, respected, or admired they are as a leader.

Getting Things Done … or Just Being Bossy?

Power adds to influence, but according to the experiences of Sheryl Sandberg and other power women, successful men in leadership roles are much more likely to earn respect than women in high-ranking positions are. Confident, decisive, and in-control men are described as assertive, Sandberg says, "but women displaying the same traits are labeled bossy, aggressive, or bitchy." Assertiveness is viewed positively in men yet negatively in women, and Sandberg believes that women are being punished for exhibiting leadership traits: "Ambitious, hard-charging women violate unwritten rules about what's acceptable social conduct—and this is holding women back." Those unwritten rules revolve around outdated traditional gender stereotypes. Women are encouraged to be polite, accommodating, and nurturing, and their role should revolve around cooking, cleaning the home, and taking care of the children.

"If more women are in leadership roles, we'll stop assuming they shouldn't be."—Sheryl Sandberg

---

YouTube CEO Susan Wojcicki knows a thing or two about making things happen. She's an innovative leader who continues to push Google and YouTube in new directions, placing her at No. 6 on *Forbes*'s 2018 World's 100 Most Powerful Women list, *and* she's the mother of five children. She is a successful woman, but she agrees with Sandberg, commenting that despite her achievements, she's had her abilities and her commitment to her job questioned, and has been overlooked, excluded from industry events and social gatherings, ignored by outside leaders in meetings who chose to address her more junior (male) colleagues instead, and frequently interrupted or spoken over in the boardroom. Both Sandberg and Wojcicki have had to overcome these unwritten rules by using their attitude of success to change the attitudes of others around them.

Leading with Power

Powerful women learn how to command a room using positive body language, they learn to push themselves as they continue to push boundaries by stepping out of their comfort zone, and they learn to silence self-doubt by maintaining a growth mindset. The experiences of Sheryl Sandberg and Susan

Wojcicki highlight the difficulties facing women in executive roles, but the attitudes they have adopted, it becomes clear that successful women share several traits that equip them to lead with power.

Women Who Lead with Power Are ...

Passionate about what they do. It's often said that successful people do what they love and love what they do. Melinda Gates was one of the first women to hold a technical role at Microsoft, Marissa Mayer was Google's first female engineer, and Amelia Earhart was the first woman pilot to fly solo across the Atlantic. These women didn't set out be influential firsts—they were simply pursuing their passions. They chose to study and work hard to become the best they could be in the field that inspired them, and they owned their success.

Willing to step out of their comfort zone. When asked for the secret to her success, Melinda Gates said, "Get comfortable being uncomfortable." Successful women know that having the courage to keep pushing themselves is the only way to achieve their true potential. Marissa Mayer puts it this way: "I always did something I was a little not ready to do. I think that's how you grow."

Not afraid to speak up, even when their opinion is unpopular. Not everything a leader has to say will be popular, but women who lead with power are not afraid to speak their mind, initiate tough conversations, or hold their own in a debate. Maggie Kuhn, activist and founder of the Gray Panthers movement, once said, "Speak the truth, even if your voice shakes."

Comfortable with standing out. As Melinda Gates once said, "The world doesn't need more people who think and act the same—so resist the temptation to conform to what's around you." Women who lead with power recognize their strengths and the differences they have that make them stand out, and they choose to own and promote those abilities rather than modestly trying to blend in.

Try This

The most successful leaders inspire others to follow their lead. These seven tips from experienced leaders will help you to develop your ability to lead with power.

1. **Lead by example.** Set the tone and others will follow your example. Be punctual, dress appropriately, be courteous, and lead through showing rather than telling.

2. **Be a skilled communicator.** Communication is a two-way street. Effective leaders make sure they are heard and understood, but they also listen to others.

3. **Set limits.** Set clear boundaries in place and stick by them. Making clear what you will and will not tolerate leaves no room for confusion.

4. **Demonstrate humility.** Leading with power is not about making yourself the center of attention. A great leader gives credit where it's due.

5. **Trust your team.** A successful leader trusts her team to do what they do best; they avoid micromanaging.

6. **Use head *and* heart**. Use your head to make the best decisions for the company, but use your heart to develop healthy workplace relationships. Successful leaders are emotionally intelligent and sensitive to the needs of others.

7. **Always keep improving**. A great leader never stops learning. Seek mentors, learn from the experiences of others, and embrace every opportunity to learn new things.

ATTITUDE 9:

Lose the Perfectionist Mentality

"I am not superwoman, and that's okay."

Aiming high and striving to be the best you can be is a good thing, but your best and perfection are not one and the same. The psychological definition of perfectionism is defined as "a person's striving for flawlessness and setting excessively high performance standards, accompanied by overly critical self-evaluations and concerns regarding others' evaluations."

If you have a perfectionist mentality, doing a good job is never enough. Not even excellence is good enough to satisfy your excessively high standards, and your overly critical inner voice will tell you that you could have done better. Almost perfect equates to failure in your mind, and nothing other than total perfection is acceptable in any area of your life. This means that a perfectionist mentality effectively prevents you from experiencing success.

Not Being Superwoman

There's a great amount of pressure on successful women to be successful in *every* aspect of their lives. A perfect performance in the workplace is expected to be matched by a perfect home and family life, thereby perpetuating the belief that women in executive roles must strive to "have it all." A woman who chooses her career over her family faces criticism, but if she chooses to devote more time to her family, her commitment to her career is questioned. The potential to feel guilty one way or the other is enormous, so when perfectionism is added to the mix, it becomes a recipe for disaster.

> *"Trying to do it all and expecting that it can all be done exactly right is a recipe for disappointment. Perfection is the enemy."*
> *—Sheryl Sandberg*

Dr. Jennifer Duong says, "The idea that fulfilling all of your roles and responsibilities to perfection will lead to a lifetime of happiness and balance is not realistic, nor should it be. Instead of feeling fulfilled, you can find yourself feeling stressed, anxious, and chronically fatigued."

Not Having It All

When Susan Wojcicki first joined Google, she was four months pregnant. Now the mother of five children and the CEO of YouTube, she still manages to get home in time for dinner with her family every evening, making it appear that she has it all. Melinda Gates has three children and is currently ranked #3 on *Forbes*'s World's 100 Most Powerful Women list; Sheryl Sandberg is Facebook COO and has two children; Marissa Mayer, who has three children, gave birth to twins while CEO at Yahoo!; Mary Barra is the CEO of General Motors and mother to two children … the list goes on. But do these powerful women really have it all, and do they set an unattainable standard of perfection for women in the workplace?

"Just because you can have and do it all doesn't necessarily mean you should," says Dr. Jennifer Duong. "It's important to identify what you personally want and what is important to you. Superwoman is a fictional character, not a role model, and trying to be her isn't sustainable or healthy." This is a sentiment wholeheartedly shared by the power women listed above. Sheryl Sandberg believes that the expression "having it all" must be dropped and that women should be encouraged to focus on having what matters to them, whatever that may be. Susan Wojcicki agrees, noting that creating a healthy work–life balance applies to everyone, not just women who have children. "Success is not based on the number of hours that you've worked," Wojcicki says. "If you are working 24/7, you're not going to have any interesting ideas." Mary Barra adds, "We need to find the opportunity not to do everything, but to do the important things."

Not Doing Everything: Making Choices and Doing What Matters

Women in leadership roles are focusing on what's important to *them* and making choices that help them to achieve *their* goals, and they encourage all women to do the same. It's not about being perfect; it's about being your best, doing your best in what matters to you, and accepting that you don't need to be perfect to be a success.

Losing the Perfectionist Mind-set

Perfectionism can hold you back. In a perfectionist mind-set, fear of failure can prevent you from trying new things and pushing boundaries. When you lose the perfectionist mentality, you open yourself up to a world of opportunity and you realize that failure is never final, and success is never ending. Losing the perfectionist mentality begins and ends with learning to be less self-critical and accepting that no one is perfect, that everyone makes mistakes, that it's okay not to be liked by everyone, that everyone has bad days, and that doing your best *is* good enough.

Try This

Power women do their best—they're not held back by a perfectionist mentality. These three strategies are tried-and-tested approaches that can help you to break free from perfectionism.

1. **See the bigger picture.** If you have a perfectionist mentality, it's all too easy to get caught up in tiny details. This can lead to several hours being spent on a task that should have taken no more than half an hour. When you find yourself getting bogged down, stop and ask yourself:

   Does this really matter right now?

   Will this still really matter tomorrow, or next week?

What's the worst that could happen if I don't do it this way?

Is the worst that could happen really that bad?

2. **Get some perspective.** When you judge yourself harshly against your high standards, take a step back and ask yourself: What would I say to a friend if they were judging themselves in this way? Sometimes it takes a different perspective to realize that you are being overly self-critical.

3. **Set Realistic Standards**: Understand that setting realistic standards does not mean having to lower your standards. A realistic standard is one that will allow you to be good enough or do a good enough job without taking over your life and preventing you from spending time on other things that matter. Adopt this approach by **compromising.** Ask yourself: What less-than-perfect standard am I able to tolerate on this task?

By compromising, you learn to accept that doing your best does not mean striving for perfection. As Sheryl Sandberg says, "Done is better than perfect."

ATTITUDE 10:

Keep Going—Grit, Determination, and Perseverance

> *"Champions keep playing until they get it right."—Billie Jean King*

Getting to the top in any field takes grit, determination, and perseverance. These traits, along with passion and a willingness to work hard, create what's known as a winning mentality. In his 1984 book *The Psychology of Winning*, Denis Waitley describes true winning as "no more than one's own personal pursuit of individual excellence. You don't have to knock other people down or gain at the expense of others. 'Winning' is taking the talent and potential you were born with, and have since developed, and using it fully toward a goal or purpose that makes you happy."

Successful women recognize their talent, and they use it to realize their full potential. They set goals and pursue their own visions of success, but crucially, they persevere, always pushing themselves to be more of the person they aspire to be and do more of the things they feel most passionate about achieving.

First Lady

One such example of a successful woman pushing hard to be and do more is Hillary Clinton. She became known to the world as the First Lady of the United States but, politics aside, she's a woman who has pushed for many other firsts in her successful career. She was the first student ever to give a commencement speech at Wellesley College. She was the only female member of the team investigating President Nixon's impeachment. She claimed five more female firsts in her law career, and then became the first woman to be sworn in as US Senator from New York as well as the first former First Lady to be elected into office.

Hillary Clinton's capacity to push boundaries and achieve "first woman" status at each new stage of her career is something she has in common with many more power women throughout history. They share an attitude of grit, determination, and perseverance, and they see no limit to their potential achievements. Successful women keep pushing and keep growing, never allowing setbacks or failures to stop them in their tracks. They learn from setbacks and they try again, making whatever changes are necessary to keep moving in the direction of their goals. They keep playing until they get it right.

True Grit

Grit is a trait that we often associate with dogged determination, but psychology professor Angela Duckworth believes that true grit is a combination of perseverance and *passion*. Based on her research, Duckworth has concluded that determination alone is not enough to help someone achieve a goal if the goal is not something they feel passionate about achieving. This is something many successful women have demonstrated.

> Dona Sarkar failed her computer science course, but she recognized her passion, talent, and potential, and tried again; Oprah Winfrey was demoted from news coanchor to "morning cut-ins" in her early TV career; J. K. Rowling's manuscript for *Harry Potter and the Philosopher's Stone* was famously rejected by 12 publishers before being accepted by Bloomsbury; and Arianna Huffington, President and Editor-in-Chief of the Huffington Post Media Group and author of 13 books, had her second book rejected 36 times.

These women persevered in pursuit of their goals, but it was their passion that allowed them to succeed—their grit. "When you have a goal you care about so much that it gives meaning to almost everything you do," Duckworth says, "grit is holding steadfast to that goal. Even when you fall down.

Even when you screw up. Even when progress toward that goal is halting or slow."

Characteristics of Grit

All successful women share a passion for what they do, but research has identified five characteristics that are common across all people with grit.

Courage. Successful people are not afraid of failure, and gritty people accept failure as part of the learning process.

Conscientiousness. Gritty people are achievement-oriented, meaning they work tirelessly to complete a task or project and they work hard at doing a good job.

Endurance. Gritty people set long-term goals and commit to seeing them through. They are prepared to do whatever it takes for as long as it takes, and they remain focused on the long-term vision.

Resilience. Gritty people demonstrate resilience through optimism, confidence, and creativity. In simple terms, they have an underlying belief that things will work out and the capacity to move on and try again even when they don't.

Seeking excellence, not perfection. Gritty people prioritize progress over perfection. They strive to grow, move forward, push boundaries, and be the best they can be. Excellence does not require perfection.

Powerful women demonstrate these characteristics in everything they do, but they are traits that can be learned, developed, and practiced by anyone. With grit, determination, and perseverance, you, too, can achieve any goal and any level of success you aspire to.

Try This

Angela Duckworth recommends taking the following four steps to help you identify the goals you feel most passionate about and develop the grit you need to achieve them.

1. **Pursue passions and interests.** Thinking about the things that interest you is only the beginning. Angela recommends getting out

and trying things to get hands-on experience before deciding whether it's a goal you feel you can commit to achieving. You need genuine passion to develop the grit it takes to see something through.

2. **Get started.** It takes dedicated practice to develop skills. Feeling passionate about doing something makes it much more likely that you'll keep doing it, but it's only by *doing* that you can progress and improve.

3. **Find motivation through purpose.** True grit comes through finding meaning in what you do. Successful women are purpose-driven. Be clear on *why* you are working toward a goal, and draw on that reasoning to motivate and give purpose to your actions.

4. **Keep believing.** Maintain a positive mental attitude. Develop a growth mind-set to help you deal with setbacks. Successful women believe things can always get better because they can always take the action necessary to make change happen.

These steps tie in with the belief of legendary basketball coach John Wooden. He observed that the greatest achievers in the world, not just in sport but in all aspects of life, all share two common habits: **they give themselves credit where credit is due**, and **they relentlessly pursue improvement.**

Recognize your talents and potential, work hard at developing them, celebrate your every success and achievement—and **keep going**. Be relentless in your pursuit of excellence, and never give up on the goals that feed your passion.

Final Note

The overriding message in this book is that power women are not superhuman. Power women do things differently because they have *learned* how to do things differently—and you can, too. Learning how to do those things does not require extraordinary levels of intelligence, talent, or skill; it takes nothing more than developing an attitude of success.

Success is a decision, not a gift, so your journey to success begins when you make the decision to pursue your dreams and achieve your goals. However, there's no such thing as overnight success. The successful women quoted in this book did not wake up one morning to find themselves at the top of their game. They worked hard to earn their positions, and they did it by adopting the 10 attitudes set out in this book—attitudes that you can now learn, develop, and put into practice to achieve your own success.

All of us are different, and the women featured in this book all have different personalities, but all power women share the same successful attitudes. You may already recognize some of these attitudes in yourself, and you can continue building on them to ensure that you achieve the success you've always wanted.

Now is the time.

Action and perseverance are the most essential elements of achieving success. What action do you need to take to develop the attitudes shared by all power women? Make the decision to succeed, and begin now. Success takes time; it's a process that requires the accumulation all of the attitudes outlined in this book, but the surest way to get from where you are now to where you want to be is simply to begin.

Want more Success?

Visit our website at visit our website at www.powerladieshub.com for more excellent resources.

Please help other women learn the habits of success and leave us a review.

Thank you!

NOTES

NOTES

NOTES

NOTES

NOTES